**G-RAFFIX** *BOOKS*
5380 SW 3rd St.
Plantation, FL 33317
www.G-raffixArtsAndDesign.com
E-mail: info@g-raffixartsanddesign.com

First published by G-raffix *Books*, 2014

The rights of Admir Serrano as author have been asserted in accordance with the Copyright, Designs and Patents Act 1988.

**International Cataloguing Information in Publication**
Serrano, Admir
Out and About / Admir Serrano - Miami - Florida - US

For information about bulk discounts or to purchase copies of this book, please contact G-raffix Books at 954-240.1603 or info@g-raffixartsanddesign.com

Design: Mauro Faria dos Santos

Manufactured in the United States of America
10 9 8 7 6 5 4 3 2 [1]

90p;
ISBN 978-0-9913357-0-1 - Paperback
ISBN 978-0-9913357-1-8 - E-book
ISBN 978-0-9913357-2-5 - E-pdf

# OUT *and* ABOUT

### HOW TO HAVE CONSCIOUS OUT-OF-BODY EXPERIENCES

ADMIR SERRANO

**G-raffix** *books*

Florida

# OUT *and* aBOUT

## HOW TO HAVE CONSCIOUS OUT-OF-BODY EXPERIENCES

# ADMIR SERRANO

Author of *The End of Death*

*This book is dedicated to the most adventurous among us—those willing to explore the reality of our duality, of the unimpeachable fact of the existence of the Spirit and its ability to rise above and live beyond.*

# Contents

"OBEs have been reported throughout history by individuals from all walks of life…They were known to the (ancient) Egyptians, the North American Indians, the Chinese, the Greek philosophers, the medieval alchemists, the Oceanic peoples, the Hindus, the Hebrews, and the Moslems." — Michael Talbot, author of *The Holographic Universe*.

# Prologue

We are immortal beings. We never stop living. When we are awake, we live the physical life we came to Earth to experience. When we are sleeping, the body rests and we, as Spirit, rise up and go on to live, for a little while, the Spiritual life, which is our true life.

Our earthly existence is composed of two modes of living. When we are awake, functioning in the physical body, we obey the physical laws of gravity. We are not able to move around as freely as we would like. The weight of our physical body and the slow vibrations of the material world restrict our movements and impair our latent spiritual capabilities.

When we sleep we free ourselves from the ties that bind us to the physical body and to physical reality. Gravity loses its grip and we take flight, and for a while we regain our natural freedom. We take a break from physical life and return to the nonphysical or Spiritual realms for a few hours.

Our nightly dreams are signs of the continuity of our life and our immortality. Even if our body is knocked out cold in bed, we are alive and quite busy. We, as Spirit, are independent of our physical body. Awake, we use the body to function in physical reality, which requires a coarser instrument to interact with other physical things. As Spirit, we are free.

One day, sooner for some and later for others, the physical body will die and we will be free much longer than just a few hours every night. We will continue living; we will continue being our own selves, our own individuality albeit as Spirit, in a subtler nonphysical reality, which is nothing more than a finer dimension within our own physical world.

Out-of-body experiences (OBEs) are glimpses of our future nonphysical life. As we sleep and dream every night we are preparing ourselves for the ultimate OBE that will befall each one of us when our body dies. Learning to become aware when we are out of the body, which happens to all of us every night, will afford us greater control and enjoyment both in our nightly excursions as we sleep and after the final OBE when our earthly journey is over.

Now let's see how we can do it.

# Chapter One

## What an OBE Feels Like

*A* brief note before we begin. Throughout this guide I will use the terms spirit, spiritual energy, and spirit body as the immortal portion of us that leaves the physical body. But you can understand it as consciousness if you prefer or feel more comfortable with this term. Astral projection and projection of consciousness are terms synonymous of out-of-body experiences. As a wise man once said, use whatever word you want, as long as you understand each other.

I have had hundreds of conscious OBEs in the past twelve years, but there was one which was the most complete. This OBE involved pretty much every aspect of a full blown experience. You may have had such an experience yourself, and might recognize some or all the features I will be relating. For those of you not yet conscious when you are out of your body at night, this will help you get acquainted with some of the sensations you might experience as you become proficient at consciously leaving your body. Since this is a guide to teach how to induce conscious OBEs, I ask you to notice what I did to accomplish it. And if I was able to succeed, so will you.

Now we begin…

I had a feeling that night I could induce a conscious OBE. It was about eleven when I went to bed. I lay in a prone position and made myself as comfortable as I could; my arms rested at my sides and the palms of my hands were facing down. The first thing I did was to quiet my mind of mundane thoughts; the day was over, challenges of my physical life had been dealt with so now I could, for a few hours, experience in advance the nonphysical life each one of us will experience when we leave earthly life for good.

Next I concentrated on relaxing, mentally suggesting that every part of my body relax. My objective at that point was to achieve the vibrational state. The vibrational state enables easier exit of the spiritual energy from the physical body. You might have had this experience spontaneously. It happens to many people during sleep, though they might not know what it means. I will tell you what it is so the next time you feel the vibrational state you can use it to induce an OBE of your own.

It is an inner vibration that feels like a generalized tingling throughout the body, like you are receiving a mild electric shock. But there is no pain associated with it. Normally the vibrational state precedes an OBE, but it isn't necessary to achieve the vibrational state to have an OBE; in fact, most often our out-of-body experiences happen without these vibrations. However, when trying to induce an OBE, reaching the vibrational state can be a conduit to bringing about the experience. The vibrational state can also be felt when we return to the physical body rather than when we leave it, as part of the spiritual energy which left the body re-enters the physical organs.

At the height of the vibrational state the spiritual energy begins to withdraw, often from the extremities—toes, feet, legs and so on up. These were my experiences; perhaps other OBErs may have them differently. As the spiritual energy withdraws, it rolls up like a snowball, accumulating more energy and moving upwards. When we are keenly focused on what is happening, we will notice that as energy is removed from a certain part of the body, that part becomes cold and rigid. By the time all the energy has withdrawn and is accumulated in our head, the entire body becomes rigid, or cataleptic, not unlike a corpse, with the difference that the organic force keeps the body alive as we, in our spirit body, get out for a while.

Sleep and dream researchers who monitor patients in their labs throughout the night know of this rigidity—also called sleep paralysis—

that occurs in the body of their subjects. The explanation given by these researchers is that some kind of subconscious mechanism exists that paralyzes the body in order to prevent us from acting out our dreams. What they mean by this?

Pretend you have a guest you don't like too much coming unexpectedly from afar to spend two days with you. You don't like the idea, but end up accepting it out of kindness. And those two days turn to two weeks with no sign of ending. Your hints that it's time for him to hit the road fall on deaf ears. You begin to feel like strangling your unwanted guest. One night you dream you are indeed strangling him. If your body weren't paralyzed, say dream researchers, you would get up, sleepwalking, and would strangle your guest for real.

With the onset of catalepsy in an OBE, breathing and heartbeat rates diminish. This is also observed in dream and sleep labs, in the Non-REM stages of the sleep cycle, which I will discuss shortly. With our body now cataleptic and cold and our spiritual energy accumulated in the head, we are ready to get out, or abruptly end the entire process if fear or doubt takes over. So the key is to give firm mental suggestions to exit. "I'm out of my body now" or "Now I leave my body", or other words to that effect.

At this point of the experience we feel a sort of pressure in our head, and may hear a buzzing or whooshing sound, sometimes we hear voices, laughs, music or our name being called.

Or a warning!

One night I was about to exit the body when I felt my deceased mother by the side of my bed. Her loud and clear voice rang in my head. "Admir, go back, don't leave now!" So back I went. When mother dear tells you, you obey, whether she is in physical or nonphysical life. Later that night I left without a problem, but for some reason that moment wasn't appropriate. We're never alone during out-of-body experiences—or in-body experiences during our waking hours; loved ones who passed on are always overlooking and protecting us, and so are our spirit guides. We're safe.

In the height of the pressure in the head, we sense that something wants to eject. But we don't lose our cognitive abilities—thinking, reasoning, making decisions and so on. Since our consciousness is still physically focused, we remain aware of our body and our physical environment—the bed we're laying in, our room etc.

The longest part of inducing a conscious OBE is to establish the vibrational state. Sometimes it takes just a few minutes, sometimes much longer, or we may not even be able to induce one at that particular time.

In this OBE it took me about fifteen minutes to induce the vibrations. Prior to this experiment I had fixed my mind to visiting my sister in São Paulo, Brazil, my native country, over 4,000 miles from Miami. It had been about nine years since I had seen her last.

*Pop!* I was out! Out of my body, out of my room, out of Miami! Four thousand miles away in a blink of an eye, or faster. I found myself outside the front door, down a flight of stairs on the side entrance. I recognized the place immediately, since I had lived in that house before. But I looked around for other signs to verify. During a conscious out-of-body experience it is important that we take time to study the environment we are in, so that we know whether we're in a physical or nonphysical dimension. Normally we don't have control where we go once we're out, and since OBEs are training sessions for physical death, the more we learn from them the easier our re-adaptation will be when we're back in the spiritual world for good.

The door in front of me had solidity only when I was in my physical body, since we would be vibrating at the same rate, but not when I was in my subtle body. I knew it posed no obstacle to my entrance. I passed through the door as though it were wide open and went to my sister's bedroom. There are two bedrooms in the house, but somehow I went straight to the one she was in. Though she was single and lived alone, I saw two bodies in her bed—both hers. The physical grounded to the bed, and the spirit counterpart floating about a foot above it.

I was standing by her bedroom door, looking at her—the two of her. There was something that drew my attention. Both heads, the physical and spiritual, were wrapped in a sort of white bandage. In a diving motion I floated over to her. She was awake in her spirit body. I embraced her and told her I missed and loved her. I was in a heightened state of lucidity, knowing that I was out of my body, and that my physical body was lying in my bed in Miami. Thus I told my sister insistently that she wasn't dreaming; I was really there visiting her. I told her as well that I would call in the morning to ask if she remembered my visit.

As we visited I was curious about the bandage on her heads, but somehow didn't ask her about it. After returning to my body I spent some time mentally reliving my experience so that I would remember it entirely. I did call her in the morning, but she didn't remember anything. And I forgot to comment about the white bandage.

My sister has suffered from migraine headaches since she was nine years old. And it grew worse as she became an adult. About two years after my out-of-body visit I went to Brazil and stayed in her house. She was often asleep when I came home at night; so I would see her in the morning. One of those mornings as I walked past her bedroom I noticed the door ajar and peeked in. To my great surprise I saw her head wrapped in a white bandage, exactly as I had seen it during that OBE visit. I asked the reason for the bandage and she told me that when her migraine was really bad wrapping it tightly relieved the pain and helped her get some sleep. I asked her how often she did that, "Quite often", she replied. I then told her I had seen her head like that when I had visited her out of my body.

You noticed the striking difference between my experience and my sister's. I induced my own exit from the body and travelled from Miami to São Paulo, completely lucid during the entire journey. She was also out of her body but didn't know it and didn't go anywhere. Had she known or was she interested in learning how to induce a conscious OBE, she could have enjoyed more our astral visit. Not only that. She could enjoy the moments of freedom she has every night travelling to other realms of existence and acquiring conscious knowledge of the continuity of life after bodily death.

And you can learn it as well. Now let's see how…

*Chapter Two*

# The Dynamics of Sleep

W e sleep in cycles. Each sleep cycle lasts from ninety to about one-hundred-ten minutes. We normally have six to seven cycles every night depending on how many hours we sleep, plenty of opportunity to fly around.

Sleep and dream researchers have classified sleep periods as stages. The first stage is called N1, a transition between the wake and sleep states. *N* means non-REM, meaning there is no rapid eye movement during this stage. I will explain REM in a bit. N1 is also known as the hypnagogic state (from the Greek *hypn*, sleep and *agogos*, induction). Twitching, vivid images, falling sensations, our name being called are some characteristics of this stage. N1 stage is also conducive to finding solutions to problems and obtaining creative ideas. Thomas Edison, the scientist who lighted up the world with his invention of the light bulb, had a habit of napping in his lab to use the hypnagogic state to find creative ideas for inventions. Over one-thousand inventions are registered under his name.

The hypnagogic state is also very propitious to induce conscious OBE. I have had many successful ones from this stage. According to sleep and dream research we spend about 5% of the sleep cycle in this stage, the shortest of the cycles. Brain waves activity in this stage is characterized by alpha waves, 7.5 to 14 Hertz or cycles, per second.

The next stage, called N2, is the longest, about 50% of the sleep cycle. You remember in my experience in Chapter One that as I felt the spirit energy leaving a certain part of my body, that part became cold, and that breathing and heart rate also slowed down. Sleep and dream researchers have recorded such biological changes on their subjects when N2 set in, as they monitored their body activity during sleep.

N2 shows spurts of distinctive brain waves called Sleep Spindles and K-complexes, 12 to 14 Hz, which are different from the regular beta waves of the waking state, and alpha, theta and delta of the sleeping state. Anomalous brain activities have also been recorded during specific OBE experiments in labs at Duke University and the University of California at Davis, coinciding with the moment the subjects reported leaving the physical body to reach the assigned target.

Next is N3, the deepest stage of sleep, characterized by slow delta waves, .5 to 4 Hz per second. This stage may last up to 20% of the sleep cycle, and it is where parasomnias occur. Examples of parasomnias are sleep-walking, teeth-grinding, night terrors (not to be confused with nightmares), bed-wetting when we were children, and one that could get you in trouble

if you're cheating on your spouse or partner—
somniloquy, or sleep-talking.

Following N3 comes the last stage of the
cycle, called REM, an acronym for rapid eye
movement. This stage was discovered and the
term coined by dream research pioneer Eugene
Aserinsky in the early Fifties. Aserinsky used to
wire his eight-year old son to monitor his brain
waves and eye movements as the boy slept.
In REM the eyes move rapidly underneath
the eyelids, as though the person is watching
something that is happening. Because subjects
tend to remember their dreams more often
when aroused during REM activity, dream
researchers believe that this is when dreams
are happening. In this stage the body is also
rigid, cataleptic, which is, as you remember,
supposedly to prevent us from acting out our
dreams, according to dream researchers.

REM stage can last up to 25% of the cycle, or
longer as the night progresses and we're close to
awakening. This stage is also called paradoxical
sleep because of its characteristic brain waves
—beta waves—he same rapid waves our brain
produces when we are awake and active. During

the first cycles of sleep REM periods are shorter, and deep sleep longer. As the night progresses and the body rests the trend reverses. REM stages become longer and deep sleep shorter, perfect for the induction of conscious OBEs.

Physiologically the REM stage is the opposite of N2; body temperature, breathing, and heartbeat increase. Dreams in the REM stage can be very vivid and even lucid, i.e., we awake in our dream and can make conscious decisions as we would if we were awake in physical life. Lucid dreams, as I will explain later, can be a springboard to a conscious OBE.

The transition from REM sleep to the awaking state is called hypnopompic, opposite of hypnagogic, in the beginning of the cycle. The hypnopompic state is characterized by lingering dream images and drowsiness, also an excellent condition to induce a conscious OBE. In fact, many of the experiences we refer to as dreams are memories brought back from an OBE as we return to the body and reactivate the physical brain, thus the rapid waves, and the increased body temperature, breathing and heartbeat.

I normally wake up after a REM stage is

over, and before opening my eyes or moving I replay as many dreams as I can remember. If I'm not too lazy and the dream was interesting I write it down. Dream recall is very important in exercising conscious OBE, because it helps induce lucid dreams, which in turn can be used to induce an OBE. If you get up abruptly or move after a REM period, chances that you will forget your dreams right away are great.

After a REM period we normally go back to N2 stage, skipping N1, unless we get out of bed and perform some activities which bring our brain waves back to beta waves. In this case we would enter the hypnagogic state when we return to sleep, followed by the subsequent stages, until REM completes the cycle once again.

Now that we have looked at the dynamics of sleep and dream, though briefly, let's look at some exercises that can help us have a conscious OBE.

# *Chapter Three*

## How to Have a Conscious OBE

*A*s with anything else we desire to accomplish in life, determination and perseverance are key to having a conscious out-of-body experience. We already leave our physical body every night as we sleep, even if we don't notice it, as you have seen in my sister's example in Chapter One. Our goal now is to be conscious of it so that we can have control, enjoy the experience and learn from it.

OBEs can be induced from the waking state or the sleeping state. It's easier from the sleeping state because the body is more relaxed, especially after three o'clock in the morning. Training can take place during the day as we go about our waking business, prior to falling asleep and throughout the night as we awake after each sleep cycle.

During the day we can get into the habit of making mental and verbal suggestions to help us achieve a conscious OBE as we sleep. We can also write down OBE suggestions on a piece of paper and read it every time we get a chance. The idea behind these mental or verbal suggestions is to saturate the mind with thoughts of becoming conscious during sleep. When we do so, we can recognize when we are out of our body and from there direct and control our experience. It does work, I can assure you.

For example, we could say aloud or mentally several times a day and prior to falling asleep, "I am leaving my physical body," or "I am having a conscious OBE." (You will find more details in Chapter Nine.) A technique I use during the day is to ask if I am dreaming or awake. I alternate the answers. When I say I am dreaming I add, "then I can fly." If I am in a private place I jump up. Of course, gravity pulls me back down, since I am awake, but when I jump up from the dreaming state, I do fly. And so will you.

Since flying is the most exhilarating part of an OBE, if you're a fan of Superman movies, you can watch one every night for a week or so before retiring, and put yourself in the superhero's place as he flies throughout the universe to save the day. Then prior to falling asleep pretend you are Superman and see yourself flying out of your room and out to space. Do this exercise if you wake up during the night as well.

As you go about your daily routine try to find opportunities to sit back and relax somewhere for ten to twenty minutes. In your house, your office, outdoors when you have a break, in the bus or train if you use these means of transportation on a daily basis. Close your eyes and clear your mind of any thoughts and feelings that are bothersome, replace them with thoughts and feelings of peace and tranquillity. Then relax physically, trying to relax your entire body, paying attention to the reactions that will ensue as you calm yourself mentally and physically. Depending on the depth of this relaxation you may achieve the vibrational state, at least in its initial phase. If you do, don't panic, just enjoy it. The vibrational state also works as a shield against negative energies that surrounds us everywhere. Do this exercise prior to falling asleep as well.

We are primarily mental beings—powerful mental beings. Every thought we have, every idea we conceive, and every action we take originates in the mind. If we take a sugar pill or an innocuous shot believing it is a powerful medication, we can cure diseases. This is called *placebo effect*, or *expectation effect*, as it is also referred to. The Food and Drug Administration—FDA requires pharmaceutical companies to compare a medication they want to market against a placebo. In these trials the subjects who have the disease the medication is purported to cure don't know whether they are taking the real medication or the placebo. And many are the cases where the placebo— or the subject's mental expectation—is more effective that the real medication. Side effects such as nausea, headache, and drowsiness have also followed the ingestion of sugar pills. Here the expectation was negative. Of course, such effects aren't caused by the placebo administered to the subjects, but by their mental expectation of what it can or cannot do to them.

If we can cure diseases by ingesting sugar pills, we can certainly become conscious when out of our body if we so desire! Knowing that we have such a mental power, we can harness it to enjoy the incredible experience a conscious OBE has to offer.

As you get ready to fall asleep it's important that you lay comfortably; your room should have a pleasant temperature and quietness so that disturbances are minimized. Reading about OBE before falling asleep also helps; remember, the idea is to saturate the mind. You can also write down your suggestion for the night, several times. I normally write it at least twenty times, and keep repeating it as I enter the hypnagogic state. "I am out of my body", "I know I am out of body", "I am having a conscious out-of-body experience," are some versions I have used. The hypnagogic state, the transition between the awake and sleep state we saw in Chapter Two, N1, is a wonderful moment for us to deepen the mental suggestions for a conscious OBE. Don't be surprised if you leave your body consciously at the first trial. But if you don't, even in the first week or two or in a month, don't give up. You're making progress. Keep working at it and you will achieve an OBE. The spiritual world needs all the help they can get from us when we're out, and when guides see our efforts, they lend a hand. You can be sure of it. As I said before, we're never alone.

If you awaken between cycles, you can repeat the suggestions before falling asleep again. You can also use the hypnopompic state at the end of the REM stage to induce a conscious OBE. As I mentioned earlier, after three in the morning as the body has rested and is more relaxed a conscious OBE becomes easier to induce. Some OBErs believe that sleeping with the head towards the magnetic north facilitates conscious OBE. You can try this, too. I sleep with mine towards the east, and that's no deterrent.

## Lucid Dreams

We can use lucid dreams effectively to induce conscious out-of-body experiences. In fact, many lucid dreams *are* out-of-body experiences; all we need to do is to recognize them as such. Lucid dreams differ from our normal dreams in that at one point in the experience we know we are dreaming. We become lucid or conscious in the dream. Thus we can control our actions. When I become lucid in a dream the first thing I say is "I know I am dreaming," or if it's an OBE I say "I am out of my body," followed by "I'm Admir Serrano, and live at…" I say my complete address and phone number, sometimes even my social security.

My objective is to equate the experience as much as I can with physical reality to increase my lucidity, thus gaining more control. With this technique I have attained such a heightened state of awareness during a number of OBEs that I was certain I was in the body, like I am now. When I thought about jumping up and flying I would hesitate, believing I would fall to the ground and hurt myself. In other occasions I knew I was out of the body, and thought it impossible to be so lucid and still be connected to the physical body. I was sure I had disincarnated, that is, my body had died. But I returned, as you can tell.

When I gain lucidity I look around to see where I am and if there is someone with me. If I recognize that it is a lucid dream and not an OBE, I jump up and fly, thus inducing an OBE. When I recognize that I am out of my body I normally do a reality check. I look at my hands and feet, touch my face and run my fingers through my hair, and more often than not, reach the back of my head and tug the silver cord, which is always present and stretched. I have done this hundreds of times, and not once have I failed to find the silver cord. But one day I will fail, of course, the day my body dies and I leave it for good.

# Chapter Four

## Getting Radical

*M*ental and verbal suggestions, relaxation, visualization and self-hypnosis are conducive to conscious OBEs. But you can get more radical if you want, as I have. The thirst experiment can be an almost certain exercise to induce a conscious OBE. In my experiment I induced one at the first trial, a few hours after preparation.

This experiment is as follows: You do not drink any liquid after twelve noon. So you're going to be quite thirsty by the time you go to bed at night. You can eat, of course, but the less you eat the greater the chances of success.

Before going to bed for this experiment I went even more radical. I put a pinch of salt in a tablespoon, added water, held it in my mouth for a few moments and spat it out. I then filled up a glass of cold water and set it on the kitchen counter. I got three index cards and wrote a brief instruction on each, "Jump up and fly," "Fly through the sliding door," "Go through the front door," and placed them next to the glass of water.

I turned off the kitchen light and turned on the stove light, which afforded enough clarity to read the instructions on the cards. Before I went to bed I picked up the glass of cold water and brought it to my lips, but didn't drink any. It was just a teaser. I put it down and read one of the cards. I then proceeded to my bedroom, lay down in bed and made myself comfortable. After relaxing for a few minutes I got up and went back to the kitchen. Once again I picked up the glass, brought it to my lips, didn't drink any, put it down, and read a card. For the next thirty minutes or so I repeated this procedure five or six times.

The idea behind the instructions on the index cards was that if I succeeded in leaving my body to get to the water, I'd read one of the cards and would follow the instruction—jump up and fly, fly through the sliding door or leave through the front door.

When I finally lay down to sleep I'd picture myself getting up and making my way to the kitchen, doing exactly as I had done before. I ran this trajectory in my mind several times, and fell asleep. If this wasn't mental saturation I don't know what was.

Persistence pays, I assure you! And guess what? A few hours later I felt myself leaving the physical body and walking to the kitchen, exactly as I had done when I was in the body. I went straight to the counter, tried to grab the glass of water, gave up, and proceeded to read one of the cards. I saw the cards perfectly but the words were all jumbled up, due to my limited lucidity at the moment. Conscious that I was out of my body I walked out of the kitchen, as the front door was right next to me, I crossed through it and went outside to the parking lot. I then jumped up and took flight. It was a delightful experience.

After returning to my body I got up, walked to kitchen and guzzled the glass of water.

# Chapter Five

## OBE in the Lab

*O*ut-of-body experience is a phenomenon as old as humanity. Yogis, mystics, and shamans have practiced it from time immemorial to access nonphysical realities. But OBEs aren't something restricted to a privileged few; everybody has this experience, though not everybody remembers having had one. Academic surveys on the incidence of OBE date back to 1954, with an average of 25% respondents reporting having had such experiences. When extended to non-Western cultures the results weren't too different, thus showing the universality of the phenomenon. When asked the circumstances of the experience respondents said they happened most often when they were asleep, relaxed, or dozing. So we are in the right track with our exercises.

These weren't the first studies on the subject either. Systematic studies can be traced to France in the mid 1800s. The term given to the phenomenon back then was somnambulism (not to be confused with sleepwalking), bi-location was another term used. Military engineer, historian, writer and parapsychologist Albert de Rochas and Allan Kardec, founder of Spiritism, were active investigators of the phenomenon.

But it was in America that OBEs were first tested in laboratory settings. In 1965 Dr. Charles T. Tart, a psychologist and dream researcher at the University of California at Davis, studied a woman who said she could induce conscious OBEs. You remember in my radical experiment that I wrote instructions on three index cards to read when out of body. Upon leaving my body I went to the kitchen, saw the cards, but couldn't read the instructions because I saw the words all jumbled up. I didn't see them clearly because my level of lucidity was low. Dr. Tart's subject, nicknamed Ms. Z, was given a somewhat similar task. She was instructed to leave her body and read a number that had been written on a piece of paper and placed on a ledge in the lab. Unless she was elevated a certain height, Ms. Z couldn't have access to the paper. The nights of the experiments she slept in the lab, hooked up to monitors so that bodily activity could be measured.

Early one morning she did read the number correctly while out-of-her body: 25132. Lucky guessing was considered, but when the odds against guessing correctly a random five-digit number were calculated, experimenters arrived at figure of 100,000. Prior to leaving her body, the readings of Ms. Z's brain waves on the EEG were the normal patterns of the sleep cycles. But during the moments she said she was out, waves showed a strange and unclassified drowsy state, uncommon during regular sleep. In Dr. Tart's opinion the anomalous wave patterns suggested that something more than extra-sensory perception (ESP) or guessing was involved in Ms. Z's experience.

OBE lab experiments have also been done at Duke University in Durham, North Carolina. In the early 1970s the Psychical Research Foundation, associated with Duke University, conducted a number of OBE experiments with several subjects. Now called Rhine Research Center in honor of Duke's parapsychology research pioneer Dr. J.B. Rhine, it is still active today. Rhine Research Center, of which I am a member, has recently announced that in 2014 it will resume OBE research with a focus on scientific studies of survival of physical death.

Back in the Seventies astonishing results were obtained from experiments with then Duke's psychology student Keith Harary. Keith had a natural ability to leave his body at will, making him a perfect subject. In one of the experiments Keith was to leave his body, which had been hooked up to monitors at Duke's lab, to appease his agitated kitten in a room a distance away. The kitten had been placed on a checkered board where a researcher monitored its activities.

Normally the kitten was very agitated and meowed frequently. But every time Keith said he had been projected to and played with the kitten, the researcher noted marked changes in the kitten's behaviour. It became calmer and meowed less when Keith said he had been there. In another experiment he was to project to a serpent's cage, which was normally calm when left unmolested. However, at a certain point in the experiment researchers witnessed the serpent attacking the glass wall of the terrarium, coinciding with the moment Keith said he was there teasing the snake. In another experiment Keith projected to a meditation room where random staff members had been sitting, of whom Keith had no knowledge. His task was to name who was sitting where in the meditation room. Keith got all the names and positions correct at the first trial.

The advent of Modern American Spiritualism, begun in 1848 after the Hydesville Rappings, launched a new era of spirit communication worldwide. A few years later psychic research seeking to verify or debunk such communication had been led by the brightest—and most skeptic—scientists in Europe, and then in the US. The American Society for Psychical Research was founded in 1884, in Boston, Massachusetts. Among psychic phenomena investigated by this organization is out-of-body experience. In 1972 experiments were conducted with Ingo Swann as the subject. Swann was a star psychic at the time, namely for his extraordinary clairvoyance or remote viewing abilities. In one of the experiments Swan was to leave his body and float up to peek through a small hole inside a box that had been hanging near the ceiling, and then reproduce the drawing that had been placed inside. Swan did so correctly in more than one experiment.

Both Ingo Swann and Keith Harary—among other psychics—were employed by the CIA and paid by the US government to work as 'psychic spies'. Using their ability to leave their bodies, their job was to eavesdrop on US enemies, namely the former Soviet Union, which was running its own psychic spies program. Codenamed Stargate, the program began in 1972 and ended in 1995, from the Nixon to the

Clinton Administrations. The Stargate program was conducted at Stanford Research Institute, in Menlo Park, California. Stargate psychic spies obtained important military intelligence as they lay resting in a comfortable room in the research facility in Menlo Park. Some examples are information on the Russian T-72 tank, then a brand new war machine, a Soviet underground facility where beams weapons were being tested, and a nuclear device facility in a remote location in a desert in China.

The main and the largest OBE research and educational organization today is the International Academy of Consciousness— IAC. IAC is an offshoot of the International Institute of Projectiology and Conscientiology —IIPC, founded in 1988 in Brazil by renowned psychic medium Dr. Waldo Vieira. IAC and IIPC have trained over one-hundred thousand people to induce and be conscious of their OBEs, myself included. IAC focuses on self-research, where OBErs are both the investigators and the subjects, thus gaining direct knowledge rather than relying on third party's accounts, such as conventional research relies on.

Skeptics and conventional brain scientists attribute OBE to hallucinations or dissociation, many say it is a pathology, an euphemism for illness, in this case mental illness. My health, both physical and mental, is excellent, perhaps superior to that of many such debunkers, and I can emphatically say they are mistaken. As the term implies, OBE is a phenomenon by which we—in a subtle or spirit body— leave the physical body for a while. It is not a hallucination, dissociation or mental illness. If you are an OBEr you already know it is real; if you aren't, follow the instructions in this guide and you will know for yourself.

Skeptics and conventional brain scientists are invited to try OBEs for themselves as well, of course! Then after succeeding they may join us in our efforts to debunk the debunkers to whose camp they once belonged.

*Chapter Six*

## What an OBE is Not

$S$ince they likely have not had conscious OBEs, skeptics, conventional brain scientists, psychiatrists and psychologists get confused about the OBE phenomenon. In trying to explain it in their materialistic point of view they have used terms as autoscopy, dissociation, and depersonalization as synonymous of OBEs.

Autoscopy, from the Greek "self watcher" is the experience of seeing one's duplicate body, either due to a brain injury, substance use, or without any influence at all. For instance, you are relaxing in a couch and all of a sudden you see another *you* standing next to the relaxing *you*. This is autoscopy. The locus of your consciousness is in your physical body, manifested through the brain. In an out-of-body experience or to be considered an out-of-body experience, your cognitive abilities must be transferred from the physical to your nonphysical body. And your locus of consciousness must be from your nonphysical body's perspective, not from the standpoint of the physical body.

Using the same example above… You are relaxing on a couch and all of a sudden you feel yourself out of your body. You look at the couch and see another form of you lying on it. Not yet familiar with the phenomenon, you may feel astonished and ask yourself, "What is happening to me?" Though a strange experience, you feel good, light and free. Just then you become aware that this thinking and feeling *you* is the one standing or floating outside, not the physical body lying on the couch. The physical body lying on the couch is passed out; consciousness is no longer present in it. This is an OBE. Your thinking abilities have been transferred from the physical brain to your nonphysical self. Materialistic researchers and skeptics fail to make this distinction. Knowledgeable hardcore ones may even know about this distinction. But they will stand their ground for the pathological explanation; otherwise they will have to seriously consider the existence of a nonphysical portion in all of us, and that is not an option to them. They refuse to shift paradigm, even if the one they are defending is flawed. Their reputation may be irreversibly damaged if they do. And besides, there is no research money readily available to study the human spirit, just our body parts and physical process.

Dissociation and depersonalization are other materialistic explanations for OBEs. Dissociation, if implying the meaning of the term, to disconnect or to separate, it could be acceptable, since we do disconnect and separate from the physical body during an OBE. Psychologically the terms are mostly associated with some kind of mental disorder, or traumatic experience causing the person to lose track, at least temporarily, of whom or where she or he is. Psychological conditions of both dissociation and depersonalization and their respective diagnostics are discussed in the Diagnostic and Statistical Manual of Mental Disorders—DSM—the guide followed by mental health professionals to diagnose and treat mental disorders. To be considered a mental disorder, according to the DSM, these conditions must be causing the patients a disruption in their normal functions of consciousness, memory, identity, or perception of the environment. In other words, when affected by these disorders one's normal daily functions and ordinary personal and social activities would be negatively impacted.

OBEs cause nothing of the sort. In the height of my experiences a few years ago when I would have three or four conscious OBEs a week during the night, I would get up in the morning and spend my day in such a state of bliss and lightness that I'd feel I could fly even in my physical body. My day would be so creatively productive and my interactions with family members, co-workers and friends so peaceful, nurturing, and rewarding. Could just half of the world population have such conscious experiences more often we would build a paradise on Earth. Perhaps we will do so some day. For now, let us continue leaving our physical bodies consciously and enjoying it. We are not cuckoos, even if scientists may believe we are.

Now let's see how we know we are having an OBE.

# Chapter Seven

## Signs of an OBE

*H*ow can we know that we have had or are having an OBE? There are some signs, including in our physical body.

A strong sign is the vibrational state, which I mentioned in Chapter One. As spiritual energy connected to physical molecules begins to loosen up to form the spirit body, an inner vibration is produced. If we work with it by willing out of our body when we begin to feel it, we are most likely to succeed. In case we don't want to leave our body when this happens, we can just let the vibration take its course. It's good for our health as it shakes off stagnant energies. The vibrational state may also happen when we, in our spirit body, are reentering the physical counterpart after being out and about, even if we don't remember anything.

Another physical sign is catalepsy, or sleep paralysis, also previously mentioned. Sometimes during the night we become conscious that we can't move our body. Try as we might, we can't even flicker an eyelid or move a pinkie. This is a sign that we, in our spirit body, are close to the physical counterpart but not entirely connected with it. We spend a great part of the night in the cataleptic state, even if we don't notice it, which is often the case. When in this condition, i.e., feeling our body rigid, we can give mental suggestions to exit our body completely, thus inducing a conscious OBE. Or we can just remain calm and will ourselves inside. We will reenter.

Falling sensations or falling dreams are also signs of OBE. If we pay attention to the fall, we will notice that as we are about to hit bottom we wake up, most likely with a jolt and with our heart racing. The jolt and the racing heart are consequences of our abrupt return to the physical body. Had the return been subtle, as it is mostly common, we wouldn't have felt anything as dramatic.

Another sign is a dream with extreme clarity. So vivid that we notice the most minute details, including our thoughts and emotions. We may even think that we are in physical reality. Many such dreams may involve an encounter with a deceased loved one. When we tell someone about it, we may catch ourselves saying, "but it was too real to be a dream." Here we are out of our body but not entirely conscious of it; we are enjoying a great level of lucidity or awareness, as we normally do in awaking life. Thus our statement that it was too real to be a dream. It was real, not a dream.

A sure sign that we are out of our body is a flying dream. If we are flying, we are out and about. We don't fly inside our heads; we fly out in space, either through the physical or nonphysical dimensions. I have trained to become lucid, that is, to know that I am out of my body when a flying episode starts. As I have mentioned before, to test my level of awareness I say my name and that I am out of my body, followed by my phone number and my address. This has become standard, and sometimes I include my social security number and the name of my daughters.

One occasion a few years ago I spoke the model, make, year, color and license plate of a van I owned. I doubt anyone can do this if they are dreaming! In a dream nobody can, but out of the body, anybody can. In order to attain such high level of awareness as the body sleeps, our mind must be functioning independently, not through the physical brain.

In one of my flying dreams as my body lay in Miami I landed on the sidewalk of a busy street in São Paulo, in a suburb I am familiar with from the time I lived there. It was early morning and the sun was rising, as the time there was three hours ahead of my time in Miami. To my right was an OBE companion, and to my left a Brazilian young man standing, perhaps waiting to cross the street. In a great level of lucidity— and mischievousness—I wondered if the young man could see or feel my presence. Leaning very close to his ear I yelled, "Bom dia!" (Good morning!). I don't know if he saw me or heard my voice, but he looked at my direction startled as he jumped two yards to the left, scrambling out without looking back. I couldn't help but have a good laugh before returning to my body in Miami.

In a recent flying dream right after doing my awareness check, i.e., saying my name, phone number and address, I looked ahead and saw the back of some houses next to each other, partially lighted by lamps on poles. As I flew towards one of the houses, I looked down and saw a field of tall grass underneath. The houses looked familiar but I couldn't just pinpoint where I had seen them. Just then I found myself back in my physical body. Before opening my eyes or making any movement, I ran the scene in my mind several times, from the moment I became lucid. I kept trying to remember where I had seen those houses. In the morning as I drove out of the security gate I looked to my right and saw the field of tall grass I had flown over not too long before. I drove up a little more and stopped the car, beholding the back of the houses I had just seen as I returned to my body. It was the houses in the condominium I was living at the time.

Before we fall asleep at night we can give ourselves suggestions that we will become lucid during our flying dreams. We can get into the habit of saying "Tonight I will fly and will become lucid." With patience and perseverance we will, and as we do, we can check our surroundings for our own proof that we are indeed out of our body. Thus verifying the truthfulness of the phenomenon.

OBE is a personal and wonderful experience of ascertaining on our own that we are immortal beings. As we become more proficient, we will conquer the greatest fear that humans must deal with, fear of death. "Knowledge is the antidote to fear," said Emerson. We will know that we are immortal, and will fear death no more.

## Chapter Eight

## We Will Return, Unless...

*A*s you can tell—as of this writing—I have returned to my body after every nightly outing. And so have you, if you are reading these words through your physical eyes. But there will be a day that we will not return, and that is when the body we are using now finishes its earthly term. Until then, no matter what happens out there, we will return.

Many people I know tell me that OBEs are dangerous. These are people who haven't learned to be conscious during their OBE. The day they learn, they will change their opinion. There is absolutely no danger in leaving our body. It is something that occurs naturally, like our breathing or heartbeat, even if we aren't aware as it happens. Our physical body will not die if we leave it for a while, as we do every night. Do not worry about that. For us to leave it for good the body needs to die. And it dies when we no longer need to be on the earthly plane. Generally, we, as spirit, have nothing to do with the death of the physical body; its death is caused by some organic malfunction, due to the passing of time, an illness, an accident, or some other event capable of severing its vital functions. Our nightly short absences do not sever the body's vital functions, so we return.

I began studying and researching death and dying as much as I could over a decade ago to prepare for my own physical death. I wanted to familiarize myself with the process so that my departure from Earth would be as smoothly as possible. I read some wonderful books, heard some amazing accounts, and worked with dying people. These experiences gave me a good amount of knowledge on the dying phenomenon. But because all this was third party's experiences, they didn't teach me what physical death was like. It was my spontaneous and conscious OBEs that prepared me for death. OBEs are direct knowledge of our immortality, such a powerful antidote that no fear can resist it.

Physical death is our ultimate OBE, the one in which we exit the body and return no more. And we have exited our bodies thousands of times. What we want to do now is to be conscious of the process, to gain awareness when we are out so that we can practice spirit life while still on the Earth plane. Being thus prepared, when the time comes for us to leave physical life we can step out of the body even before it takes the last breath, and don't even bother to look back. Forward we go. Forward is the way to go.

In the following chapter I will summarize and review some important key points that can help us induce conscious OBEs.

# Chapter Nine

## Key Points to a Conscious OBE

$S$ome key points have been discussed already, but due to their importance in achieving a conscious OBE we will cover them again in this chapter.

### Desire

I have said this already but rubbing it in a little deeper will do no harm. As with everything else we want to accomplish in life, wanting or desiring to do something is the first step. As Lao Tsu said, a *journey of a thousand miles starts with a single step*, and shorter ones as well. Desire is a key factor not only to induce a conscious OBE but to realize whatever dream we wish in our life. Everything we energize flourishes, anything we don't energize perishes.   Desire is the force that puts it in motion.

## Action

Desire is key, but without action it is as good as dead. No action, no reaction. This is a natural law; therefore, we can't escape it. And this goes for everything else we want to do in life, not only being aware that we are out of our body. When we desire something strongly enough and act accordingly to reach our goal we are energizing that desire, and in due time it will flourish. It is a cosmic law.

## Practice

As I said before, we all leave our physical body when we sleep every night. Our objective here is to know when we are out and also to be aware of the disconnection process as it happens so that we can have control of the OBE and enjoy the experience. Here I am referring to the suggestions and exercises I have given which are key factors to inducing a conscious OBE. I will list them again in this chapter so that you will have everything you need to be a successful conscious OBEr.

# Faith

Faith is such a powerful energy that it can carry us through the worst adversities we may encounter in life. And cure diseases too. We have seen this in the placebo effect example given in Chapter Three. Sugar pills or other innocuous component can't improve anyone's health; it's the faith of the person taking it that does the trick. Once we do our fair share of suggestions and exercises to become conscious of our OBE, let's have faith that they will work, and they will. If faith can move mountains, becoming conscious as we are out of our body is a piece of cake.

# Patience and Perseverance

Together with faith, patience and perseverance

are key factors to be nurtured as we put a desire into action and take the necessary steps to bring it to fruition. And fruition only comes when the forces we set in motion have had enough time to realize the goal we are seeking to attain. In the mean time we keep doing our part in the best manner we can. Our reward will come when we are ready to receive it. Things are working out as they should. Good things come to those who *know how to* wait.

## Mental Suggestions

Once we decide (desire) to become conscious during out-of-body experiences, our first action is giving mental suggestions. We should practice mental suggestions throughout the day as well as before falling asleep and anytime we awake at night. As I said before, the idea is to saturate the mind so that we can remember it in the dream state.

During the night only our body rests and becomes inactive; our consciousness does not, even if we don't remember anything in the morning. Mental suggestions serve to awake our consciousness during the night so that we can have control of our nonphysical activities, i.e., dreaming and leaving the body. Some mental suggestions I use are:

- *I'm having a conscious out-of-body experience*
- *I'm out of my body and I love it*
- *I know I'm out of my body*

## Exercise

Physical exercise has positive effects on our disconnection from the physical body as it alleviates tension, anxiety, and releases harmful toxins. Needless to say that exercising has a positive effect on our physical health as well. So we can't go wrong. Let's get out and pump some iron.

## Relaxation

Relaxation is the main physical factor in preparation to leave the body consciously. The more relaxed the body the easier the exit, thus our nightly escape as the body sleeps. Relaxation can be practiced during the day so that we can get into the habit, and it is a must every time we decide to engage in an OBE experiment.

During sleep we can take advantage of the natural relaxed condition of the body as we enter the hypnagogic and hypnopompic states discussed in Chapter Two. During relaxation as an attempt to leave the body it is necessary that we also give mental OBE suggestions, as discussed previously.

## Vibrational State

As we relax and give mental suggestions, we might attain the vibrational state. The vibrational state is ideal to induce a conscious OBE. Since it also occurs spontaneously during sleep, we can take advantage of it by remaining calm and motionless when we begin to feel it. And just allow it to take its course. As it is happening we must keep giving firm suggestions that we want to leave the body. We are not the body, but the spirit who controls it, therefore, we are in command.

## Falling Asleep

The hypnagogic state at the onset of sleep is very conducive to an OBE. Our body enters a natural relaxed condition and we, as Spirit that we are, begin our exit. Suggestions at this stage are very effective to gain awareness when we are out of the body. Reading about OBE prior to falling asleep is also of great help. I can assure you of that from my own experiences. You can refer back to the *Mental Suggestions* section for some examples you can use.

## Lucid Dreams

Lucid dreams, many of which are OBEs, are wonderful opportunities to practice lucidity. We dream every night, even though we may not remember our dreams in the morning. But we're lucid in just a few, if ever. So we can give suggestions to become lucid in the dream. If we can dream it, we can do it, Walt Disney has said. Being lucid in a dream means that we know we are dreaming and can make conscious decisions, like we would in the waking state. Following are some suggestions I use:

- *I will dream and will know I'm dreaming.*
- *Tonight I will wake up in my dream.*
- *When I wake up in my dream I will jump up and fly.*

## As We Awake

The hypnopompic state at the end of the last REM period, when we normally get up in the morning, is extremely conducive to conscious OBEs. I have had some amazing experiences during this stage. Week mornings I set my alarm thirty minutes before I need to get up, and use this time to do OBE experiments. I extend the practice on weekend mornings, since I'm off. In this stage our body is deeply relaxed, and our physical brain is becoming active. Images from what we have seen and done while out are still lingering. This is what I do:

- *I avoid moving, even opening my eyes.*
- *I concentrate on the most vivid images.*
- *"Go back there," I suggest. "I want to go back there."*

More often than not I see the images moving, and feel myself moving with them. As I follow, I look around, paying attention to where I'm going. I might enter a nonphysical dimension, or begin to fly somewhere. I am no longer surprised to find out that the place I end up is the same I had been prior to awakening, even meeting the same people and circumstances. So the images that had been lingering were indeed memories of what I had seen and done. If it was a dream, this couldn't happen, as in dreams nothing seems to stay stable for long.

Out-of-body experiences are not the domain of a privileged few. It is a natural phenomenon occurring to each one of us, every night of our physical lives. As such, we can educate and train ourselves to be aware when they are happening and learn how to have control and enjoy them. In doing so we will discover that we are much greater and much more valuable than we may have so far realized. In following the simple steps suggested in this guide on a regular basis, chances are that you, too, will soon be joining the growing community of conscious OBErs flying around every night. I will sure be glad to see you in outer space.

# Epilogue

$W$e are time hoppers, multidimensional beings, and we live immersed in a multidimensional reality. While in physical life we are focused on physical reality. The coarseness of our physical senses, with some exceptions, doesn't allow us to perceive subtle realities during our waking life. But at night when we put our body to rest we can and we do. When our body sleeps we close the door to the physical world we are living in and open another to the nonphysical realms from which all of us hail.

When we enter the sleep state every night we are experiencing a similar state we will find ourselves in when our body dies—a real and active life. As we sleep we learn to die. Our fear of death is unfounded. Fear of death is really fear of the unknown. We fear something when we don't know what to expect. As we learn to be conscious during our nightly excursions out of the body, we will become acquainted with the characteristics of nonphysical life. We will gain conscious knowledge of what that reality is like. And when the unknown becomes known, fear vanishes. We already know what to expect. The mystery has been revealed. We learned the truth, and the truth shall set us free.

We begin our nonphysical journey the moment we lay down to sleep. As we free ourselves from the ties of matter, we access paranormal abilities we all possess but which only occasionally manifest in the waking state. As the body rests from its daily activities, our consciousness moves from the physical to our spirit body. This transference begins in the hypnagogic state, the period between the awake and the sleep state as we retire for the night. Many of the images we see in the hypnagogic state, voices we hear, and noises we pick up are not occurring inside our brain. They belong to inner realities we are beginning to access as we, in our spirit body, move out of the physical and operate with the more refined and farther-reaching nonphysical senses.

As the body rests we begin to enjoy that which we really are—free and immortal spirits. We go places, in the physical and nonphysical dimensions. We visit old friends and relatives, both physically and nonphysically living. We learn lessons. Or we just hang out in our bedroom, sleeping as the physical body beneath. As we perform these activities, images are played in our minds, some clear, many distorted. Some are pleasant, some unpleasant. We call them dreams. We have been conditioned to call them dreams, and we have been conditioned to believe dreams are unreal. This is because in our dreams most of us play the role of spectators, passive watchers observing the incredible plays seemingly happening inside our head for unknown reasons.

But we can change our role. As we become conscious during these activities we call dream we can learn to switch from passive spectators to protagonists, active doers and actors, planning and directing our actions. In doing so we discover that the physical life we are living is but a small portion of a far greater reality we have been part of from time immemorial.

It is an awesome, rewarding feeling. This discovery is so powerful that all the limited, preconceived ideas we had of ourselves melt like a snow ball in a hot pan. We no longer try to shrink the mysteries to make them fit in the smallness of our minds. On the contrary, we expand our minds, to whatever limit is necessary, so that we can fit in it the greatness of the mysteries we are surrounded with and are an intrinsic part of.

I hope my personal experiences raised your curiosity at least to attempt to bring to awareness this greater reality we are all immersed in. You are also quite active as your body sleeps every night. All you need to do to fully realize it is to awake your consciousness when you are out.

The exercises I have shared with you here can help you achieve this awareness if you follow them. I hope you do.

To those of you daring and curious enough to try it, I'll see you tonight out there, in this glorious adventure we call life, which never ends, even if we believe otherwise.

*Not the End...*

# Bibliography

Blanke, Olaf et al., 2004. "Out-of-Body Experience and Autoscopy of Neurological Origin." *Brain*, 127.

Buhlman, William. 1996. *Adventures Beyond the Body* New York: HarperOne.

Couliano, I.P. 1991. *Out of this World: Otherworldly Journeys from Gilgamesh to Albert Einstein* Boston: Shambhala.

*Diagnostic and Statistical Manual of Mental Disorders, 4th Edition*—DSM-IV. 1994. Washington, DC: American Psychiatric Association.

LaBerge, Stephen & Rheingold, Howard. 1990. *Exploring the World of Lucid Dreaming* New York: Ballantine.

Rock, Andrea. *The Mind at Night: The New Science of How and Why We Dream.* 2004. New York: BasicBooks.

Rogo , D. Scott. *Life After Death – The Case for Survival of Bodily Death. 1986.* Northamptonshire, England: The Aquarian Press.

Schnabel, Jim. *Remote Viewers: The Secret History of America's Psychic Spies.* 1997. New York: Dell.

Sawn, Ingo. *To Kiss Earth Goodbye. 1975.* New York:

Hawthorn, 1975.

Talbot, Michael. *The Holographic Universe. 1991.* New York: HarperPerennial.

Tart, Charles T. 1968. "A psychophysiological study of out-of-body experiences in a selected subject." *Journal of the American Society for Psychical Research,* 62:3–27.

Van de Castle, Robert L. 1994. *Our Dreaming Mind* New York: Ballantine.

# Also by the author, in English

The afterlife is real, and *The End of Death* shows why and how.
Using personal experiences and examinations of first-hand accounts,
coupled with scientific evidence and academic experiments, the
author explores the phenomenon of Near Death Experience (NDE).
Compelling and eye-opening, the book is an essential read for anyone
interested in the afterlife, or those simply wanting to question why
they are here.

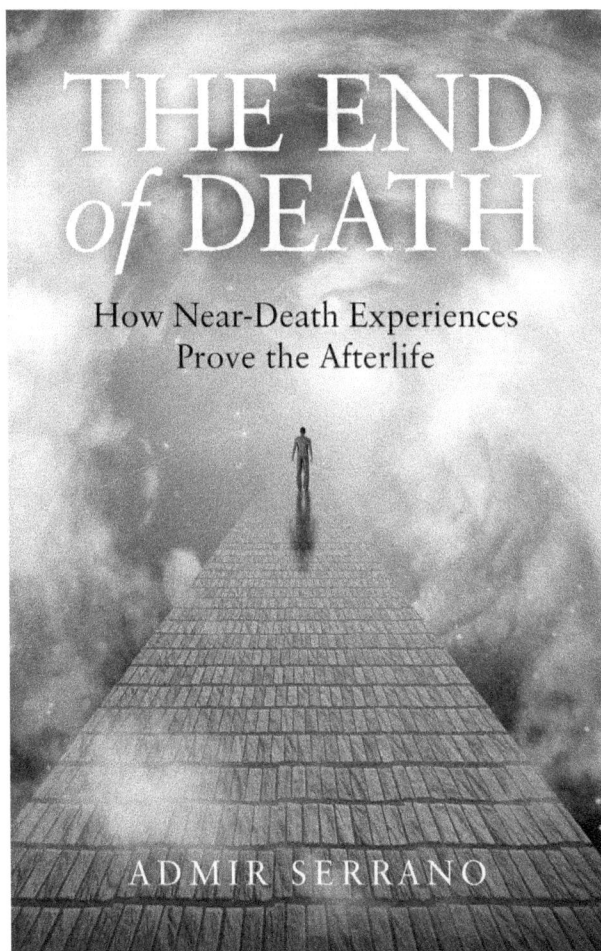

THE END
*of* DEATH

How Near-Death Experiences
Prove the Afterlife

ADMIR SERRANO

## Also by the author, in Portuguese

*Morrer Não É o Fim*
(Dying Isn't The End)

*Nos Portais do Além*
(At The Gates of Heaven)

*Sua Mala Está Pronta?*
*Seu Guia de Viagem*
*para o Além*
(Is Your Luggage Ready?
Your Travel Guide to
Heaven)

a book by

**G-raffix**_books_
954-240-1603 - www.G-raffixArtsAndDesign.com

www.ingramcontent.com/pod-product-compliance
Lightning Source LLC
Chambersburg PA
CBHW071907020426
42331CB00010B/2704